CONCISE HANDBOOK OF FLY TYING

SKIP MORRIS

PORTLAND

DEDICATION

Capturing the brevity and clarity
of a "concise handbook" proved to be a
steep task, and I put the best of myself into
accomplishing it. If I succeeded, it was in large part
thanks to the kind, generous, and supportive woman I married.
So I dedicate the *Concise Handbook of Fly Tying* to the life partner
who surpassed my wishes, my wife, Carol Ann Morris.

———————————

Published by Frank Amato Publications, Inc.
P.O. Box 82112, Portland, Oregon 97282

All photographs taken by author except where noted otherwise.
Front and Back Cover and Materials Photographs by Brian Rose.
Illustrations by Richard Bunse except where noted otherwise.
Book & Cover Design: Kathy Johnson

Printed in Hong Kong
7 9 10 8 6
Softbound ISBN: 1-57188-214-6   UPC: 0-66066-00428-4

CONTENTS

TOOLS

These are the fly-tying tools I consider indispensable. There are other optional tools that can be useful.

VISE: "Rotary" vises have jaws that rotate while holding a hook; "stationary" vises have jaws that don't. Stationary vises are the least expensive and are usually the beginner's choice, but rotary vises offer useful options.

SCISSORS: Good scissors made specifically for fly tying are a must.

BOBBIN: In my opinion, the single greatest development in fly tying. Get one and use it.

HACKLE PLIERS: There are several types of hackle pliers, and nearly all work well. They hold a hackle's tip so that the hackle may be wound.

HAIR STACKER: A hair stacker is used to even the tips of a hair bunch. The hair is loaded tips-first into the stacker, the stacker is tapped on a table top, the stacker's cap is removed, and the hair is removed, evened and ready to be tied into a fly.

HACKLE GAUGE: Consists of a post, over which a hackle is wound, and a face. The markings on the face

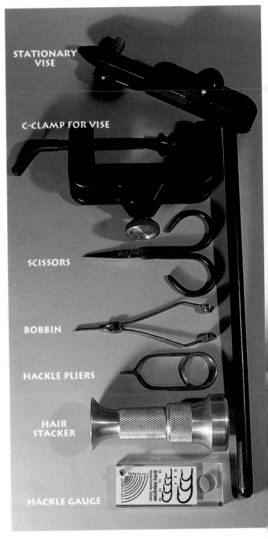

STATIONARY VISE

C-CLAMP FOR VISE

SCISSORS

BOBBIN

HACKLE PLIERS

HAIR STACKER

HACKLE GAUGE

tell the size of hook a hackle belongs with.

LIGHT: You need plenty of overhead light for tying. The adjustable-arm desk lamp remains the standard.

OPTIONAL TOOLS: Magnifier • Bodkin • Pliers • Dubbing Twister • Wing Burner • Whip Finish Tool

MATERIALS

Part of the fun of fly tying is exploring materials. Those isted and shown here are standards.

THREADS: Standard trout-fly threads are size 8/0 and 6/0. Big lies or heavy work usually require /0, or even size-A rod-thread.

TINSELS AND WIRES: Most of these are bright gold or bright silver except subtle copper wire) and are used mainly for ribs. Wires are simply wire, in various diameters. Tinsels may be flat or oval. Lead wire (or non-lead substitute) is used as weight, to get a fly down.

CEMENTS: These are used mainly to secure thread heads and finishing knots.

FURS: Both natural and synthetic furs are used in a process called dubbing."

FEATHERS: These include hackles used mainly for collars, wings, legs, and tails), primaries (also called "quills"; used mainly for wings and wing cases), various flank and breast feathers (used mainly for wings, legs, and tails), herls (peacock and ostrich; used mainly for bodies and sunk-fly wings), and pheasant tail (you name it). Downy marabou is used mainly in sunk-fly wings and tails.

HAIRS: Dense, hard hair—most hair—is used mainly for wings and tails. Spongy pocketed hair, such as deer and elk, can also be flared and trimmed to create plump, buoyant bodies and heads.

MISCELLANEOUS STUFF: Waxes are used for dubbing. Chenille is a fuzzy cord for sunk-fly bodies. Floss is a loosely gathered twine, usually for bodies. Reflective synthetic strands are used mainly in sunk-fly wings. Rubber strand is used mainly as legs. There are all kinds of gelatinous-looking synthetic rib-materials. Buoyant foam is showing up a lot, especially in dry flies.

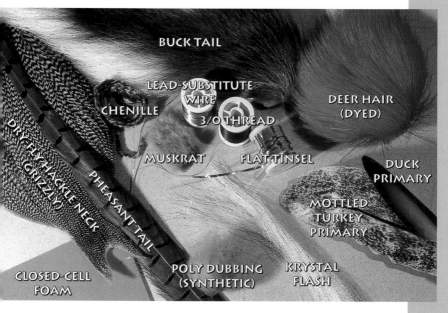

BUCK TAIL

LEAD-SUBSTITUTE WIRE

CHENILLE

3/0 THREAD

DEER HAIR (DYED)

DRY-FLY HACKLE NECK (GRIZZLY)

PHEASANT TAIL

MUSKRAT

FLAT TINSEL

DUCK PRIMARY

MOTTLED TURKEY PRIMARY

CLOSED-CELL FOAM

POLY DUBBING (SYNTHETIC)

KRYSTAL FLASH

HOOKS

After explaining fly-fishing terminology to a beginner, I often hear something like, "This stuff must be made confusing *on purpose.*" Anyone looking for evidence to support this notion need look no further than fly hooks. Nevertheless, I believe I can whittle all this down to simple, comprehensible shapes.

These are the three main considerations in selecting a hook: shank length, wire thickness, and size. But be forewarned: manufacturers don't quite agree on how all this translates into millimeters and thousandths-of-an-inch. One manufacturer's size-10, 4X long hook may be quite different from another manufacturer's size-10, 4X long hook. But in the end, the difference is usually insignificant.

SHANK LENGTH

There is a standard length for a hook's shank; everything else is measured with an "X." The longer the shank, the higher the number preceding the "X"—a 1X long shank isn't very long, but a 6X long shank is. The "X" works the same way for short shanks—a 1X short shank is slightly short, but 4X short is extreme. Regardless of shank-length, the gape and eye remain the same for all hooks of a given size.

WIRE THICKNESS

In order to make this as confusing as possible, an "X" is used to designate both shank length *and* wire thickness. Just remember that "long" and "short" refer to shank length and that "heavy" and "light" refer to wire thickness and you'll be alright.

The standard wire thickness for a given hook size is "standard wire."

The wire gets thicker as the numbe preceding the "X" goes up—1X heavy is slightly heavy while 4X heavy is heavy indeed. A 1X light hook (or 1X fine) has wire that is slightly light while one with very fine wire would be 3X light.

SIZE

Apparently the letter "X" couldn't be applied to sizing hooks, so another confusing system had to be developed; it remains in use today. The larger the number, the smaller the hook. So a size-4 hook is large, a size 12 is medium, and a size-20 is tiny. This still wasn't confusing enough, however, so someone decided that hooks larger than size 1 should be described with an "/0" ("ought") and that the larger the number, the *larger* the hook—the reverse of the smaller-hook approach. So a 4/0 hook is larger than a 2/0.

OTHER CONSIDERATIONS

The eye of a hook can be tipped up or down or it can be straight in line with the shank (see the diagram "Parts of a Hook," page 7). There are several standard shapes for the bend. Eye and bend type are mostly a matter of personal preference.

WHICH HOOKS WHERE?

Here are the most general guidelines for matching hook type to fly type. Light-wire hooks are for floating flies. Heavy wire hooks are for sunk flies. Long-shank hooks are for fish-imitations or for imitating big or long-bodied insects. Certain unusual hooks are established for specific fish, flies, or applications steelhead-Atlantic salmon hooks, bass-bug hooks, and non-corrosive saltwater hooks for example. In gen

HOOKS

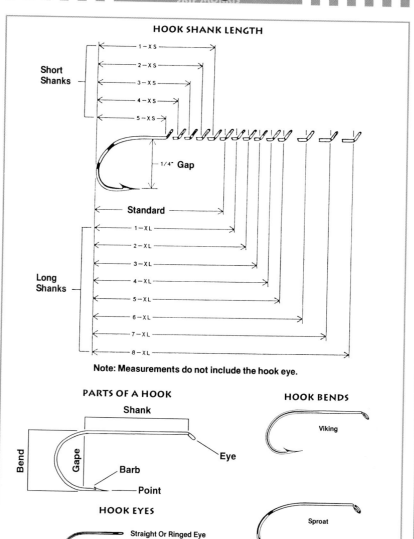

HOOK SHANK LENGTH

Short Shanks
- 1 — XS
- 2 — XS
- 3 — XS
- 4 — XS
- 5 — XS

1/4" Gap

Standard

Long Shanks
- 1 — XL
- 2 — XL
- 3 — XL
- 4 — XL
- 5 — XL
- 6 — XL
- 7 — XL
- 8 — XL

Note: Measurements do not include the hook eye.

PARTS OF A HOOK

Shank

Eye

Bend

Gape

Barb

Point

HOOK BENDS

Viking

Sproat

Limerick

HOOK EYES

Straight Or Ringed Eye

Turned Up Eye

Turned Down Eye

VIC ERICKSON

eral, simply use a hook of the shank length, wire thickness, and size called for in the fly pattern you are following (see "Pattern [Fly Pattern]," in section IV, "Techniques, Tactics, & Terms," page 12).

TECHNIQUES, TACTICS & TERMS

(LISTED IN ALPHABETICAL ORDER)

ANGLE CUTS

Once a material is tied onto a hook, one end of that material is usually cut and then bound with thread—nearly always it is best to make that cut at an angle. Blunt cuts make tiny shelves, shelves that thread slips off of or resists climbing, shelves that create gaps or bumps in fly bodies or knock hackles out of position.

Angle cuts create smooth tapers that accept thread-turns easily and provide an even foundation for bodies and hackles and anything else worked into a fly.

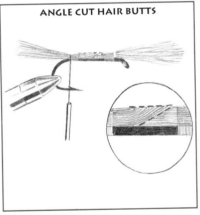

ANGLE CUT HAIR BUTTS

Where the ends of two materials meet from opposite directions—for example, the butts of wing and tail fibers—the best way to blend them is often to overlap their angle-cut ends.

BOBBIN—LOADING, HOLDING, AND ADJUSTING

To load a bobbin, mount its two nubs into the thread spool's open ends. Work the end of the thread up and out the bobbin's tube with either a loop of leader or a bobbin threader.

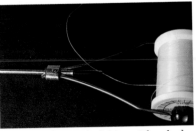

1. Threading a bobbin with a bobbin threader. Leader goes in, thread goes into the leader's loop, loop and thread end are pulled out the tube.

2. A bobbin should be held at the joint where its tube meets its arms.

If the bobbin's tension needs adjustment, do so by bending its arms with two pairs of pliers. Never stress the joint between the bobbin's arms and tube.

BROKEN THREAD

Every tier occasionally breaks thread while tying. Here's my solution:

1. Clamp hackle pliers onto the broken thread-end and let them hang. Now the thread cannot unwind.

Restart the thread, wind it back over the last few turns of the broken thread to secure everything, trim both the old end and the new, and then continue tying.

COMPONENTS OF FLIES

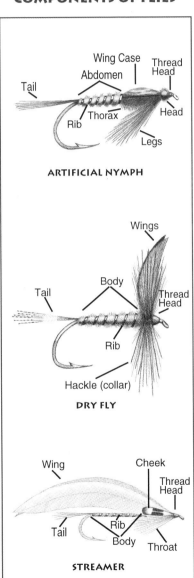

ARTIFICIAL NYMPH

Wing Case
Abdomen
Tail
Thread Head
Thorax
Rib
Head
Legs

Wings
Tail
Body
Thread Head
Rib
Hackle (collar)

DRY FLY

Wing
Cheek
Thread Head
Tail
Rib
Body
Throat

STREAMER

DUBBING

Dubbing is a technique used often in fly tying, and the fur and synthetic fibers used for it are also called dubbing, so you will be dubbing with dubbing. A stroke or two of fly-tying wax along the thread can be helpful when dubbing, though not required.

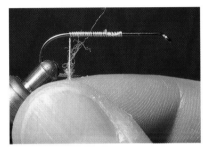

1. Hold the dubbing against the thread. Spin the dubbing and thread between your thumb and finger to form a soft rope of dubbing-layered thread.

2. Wind the dubbing-layered thread up the shank.

FLY TYPES

Flies are divided into "imitators," or "imitations," which imitate a specific insect or creature; and "attractors," which imitate nothing in particular but suggest something interesting and edible.

TONY AMATO

TECHNIQUES, TACTICS & TERMS

TECHNIQUES, TACTICS & TERMS

ARTIFICIAL NYMPH

STREAMER

DRY FLY

DOWN WING DRY FLY

BASS BUG

WET FLY

TONY AMATO

HALF HITCH

Top View

1. Raise the bobbin until the thread is horizontal. Spread your first and second fingers and bring them down until tips lay on thread.

2. Rotate your right-hand wrist until your fingers and palm point up; as you do this, raise the bobbin and then lower it to the left. The thread should cross over itself in an "X".

3. Hook the far side of the loop over the head.

4. Let the bobbin hang. Take the loop from your right-hand fingers with the first finger of your left hand.

Side View

5. Insert scissors, bodkin, or hat pin into the loop with your right-hand and remove your left-hand finger.

HALF HITCH

The half hitch is a simple fly tier's knot that can be used in place of the more involved whip finish. Two or three half hitches can finish a fly, but you will find other uses for the half hitch. These instructions are for right-handers. Once you are comfortable with the half hitch, I suggest you tackle the whip finish.

1. Create a half-hitch loop and then hook it over the thread head.

2. Pass the half-hitch loop to a hat-pin, bodkin, or scissors' closed tips (as described in the illustrations). Guide the loop closed.

HEAD CEMENT

Head cement secures the finishing knot on a fly, among other duties. There are head cements marketed specifically for fly tying, most of which are thin, but my favorite is epoxy glue. Epoxy is thick and very tough and seems to give off no vapors.

Avoid contact with any cement—every year new ailments are attributed to chemicals that are breathed or absorbed through the skin, and head cements contain chemicals.

1. Simply dab something pointed—a bodkin or round toothpick for example—into a thin cement and touch it to the finishing knot. With epoxy you need to put down a dot of it, work it around, then add more if necessary.

Stick flies whose heads are freshly coated into wood or foam. After a few minutes, check hook eyes and clear them if they are filled with cement.

LEAD

Lead is used by the fly tier for one purpose only: to add weight. Now, there are lead substitutes, which are less likely to harm rivers and fish.

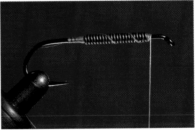

1. Wrap the lead wire tightly in consecutive turns onto the shank. Cut the ends of the lead closely. Bind the lead with tight thread-turns.

LIGHT TURN

The light-tension thread-turn, which I simply call the "light turn," is a handy quicker alternative to the pinch for tying in relatively stiff materials.

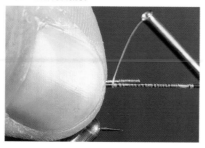

1. Simply hold the material to the hook and then take a turn of thread over it. Use only slight thread tension and no more, just enough to control the thread. Pull the turn tight and continue tying.

PALMERED HACKLE

A palmered hackle is one that is wrapped in open spirals.

PATTERN (FLY PATTERN)

A listing of materials for a specific fly, and sometimes a few instructions, is called a "pattern," "fly pattern," or "dressing." The materials are normally listed in the order in which they are called for, but this rule is often overlooked. (Sample fly patterns are shown in section VI, "Fly Patterns," page 34.)

PINCH

This technique allows you to tie in a soft material with control; obviously it is very useful.

THE PINCH

1. Hold the material to the shank. Raise the bobbin.

2. Bring the joints of your thumb and finger closer together; this will spread apart your thumbtip from your fingertip; slip the thread back between thumbtip and material.

3. Bring the thread (and bobbin) down the far side of the material as you draw the thread back between fingertip and material.

4. Widen the gap between your thumb and finger joint closing thumbtip and fingertip around the loop.

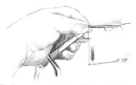

5. Pull down on the bobbin, tighten the pinch loop.

6. The material should be secured atop the hook.

Techniques, Tactics & Terms

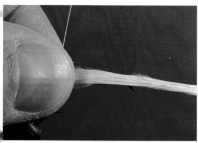

1. Performing the pinch.

2. The results of a well-executed pinch.

PROPORTIONS AND MEASURING

No fly can be considered well tied without having proper proportions. Proportions for some fly types are fairly fixed; others are largely subjective. Some fly patterns intentionally break tradition. Here are the normal proportions of the two most commonly tied flies.

As you can see from the illustrations, most parts of a fly are measured against a hook's shank, some against its gape.

STANDARD NYMPH PROPORTIONS

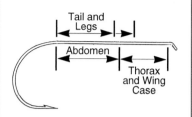

Tail and Legs

Abdomen

Thorax and Wing Case

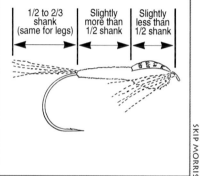

1/2 to 2/3 shank (same for legs) | Slightly more than 1/2 shank | Slightly less than 1/2 shank

SKIP MORRIS

STANDARD DRY FLY PROPORTIONS

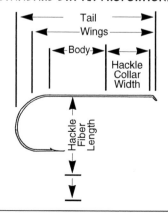

Tail
Wings
Body
Hackle Collar Width
Hackle Fiber Length

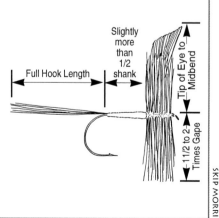

Slightly more than 1/2 shank

Full Hook Length

Tip of Eye to Midbend

1 1/2 to 2 Times Gape

SKIP MORRIS

TECHNIQUES, TACTICS & TERMS

1. Measure the material against the hook (in this case, wings are being measured against the shank and bend). Keep your eye on the measured point until the material is tied in. Often (as here) you can set the edge of your thumb at the measured point to help mark it.

RIBBING

A rib is simply a material that is spiraled up a fly, usually over the abdomen or body. A rib is thread-secured at both ends.

1. Winding a gold-tinsel rib up a nymph's abdomen.

SHAPING SPUN HAIR

After hair has been spun onto a hook (see "Spinning Hair" in this section), that hair must be shaped to a body, head, or whatever it represents. The hair can be cut with scissors or a razor blade.

1. Make the first cut along the underside of the hook.

2. Trim the sides to their final width. Trim the top.

3. Trim back the hair at its ends if necessary, and round out all the square corners.

SPINNING HAIR

Soft buoyant hairs—such as deer and elk—are often spun and shaped to produce heads and bodies on dry flies and sometimes sunk flies. A heavy thread, such as size-A rod-winding thread or single-strand floss, is usually best for this.

TECHNIQUES, TACTICS & TERMS

1. Snip a bunch of deer hair from the hide; generally, the bunch should be about the diameter of a pencil. Hold the hair near its tips and comb out the short fibers and fuzz.

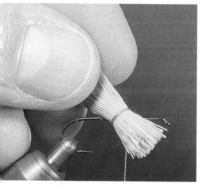

2. Trim off the tips of the hair, then hold the bunch to the near side of the shank and wind the thread around both shank and hair three times. The bunch should tip down in front and up in back.

3. Gradually tighten the thread as you gradually release the hair—spinning hair.

4. With the hair fully spun, draw it tightly back and the thread tightly forward. Add four tight thread-turns at the front of the hair. Spiral the thread forward in two or three open spirals; then spin on another bunch.

5. Push each new spun-hair bunch back into the last.

STARTING THREAD

Nearly every fly begins with starting the thread on the hook's shank.

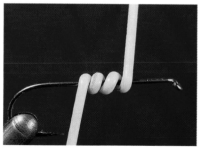

1. Make four tight thread-turns forward (towards the hook's eye). (Fly line is used here, in place of thread, for clarity.)

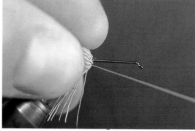

TECHNIQUES, TACTICS & TERMS

2. Make four to six tight turns back to lock the thread onto the shank. Trim the loose end of the thread and continue tying.

SUBSTITUTION

This refers to substituting a material or color in a fly in place of the original material or color. Sometimes tiers substitute because they haven't the right material on hand, but often it's because they want to alter the fly or just like playing with the possibilities.

THREAD HEAD

Most flies are completed with a thread head, which is simply a tight, tapered buildup of thread immediately behind the hook's eye. Leaving a tiny bit of bare shank just behind the eye creates a place for the thread head and insures that it will be neat, and easy to create. The triangle can also help in forming a thread head (see "Triangle" in this section).

1. Two thread heads. One is neat and tiny; the other is large but clean

and well-tapered. A matter of personal choice.

THREAD DIRECTION AND TENSION

Thread direction is easy to describe: Wind the thread *away* from you *over* the hook's shank and *toward* you *under* it.

The general rule is to use the tightest thread-turns possible, just short of breaking the thread. But occasions for breaking this rule are common: Hair wings and tails may flare too much if gathered with tight turns, foam can be cut by tight thread, and the wings for parachute hackles can be easier to form if thread-turns start light and get tighter with each thread layer. These are only a few exceptions; there are others, but follow the tight-thread rule unless there is a good reason to break it.

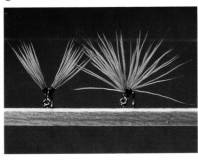

1. One exception to the tight-thread rule: the hair wings on the left are gathered neatly by the moderately tight thread-turns around each wing's base; the wings on the right are a riot for the tight turns at their base.

TRIANGLE

"Triangle" is my name for this technique, which draws materials back from the hook's eye to make easy work of forming a thread head.

1. For right-handers: bring the tips of your left-hand thumb, first finger, and second finger together. This photo shows the tiny triangular opening that results—and for which the triangle is named.

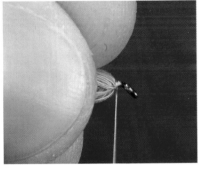

2. Slip the opening over the eye. Draw the triangle back, in turn drawing back hackles, fur, and other materials. Allow only the hanging thread-end to slip past. Build and complete a thread head, which should be easy, *now*.

WHIP FINISH

The whip finish is the standard knot for completing a fly. Some tiers use a few half hitches instead. But the whip finish is actually no more than a half hitch that forgot to stop and is as easy to execute as it sounds. (There are whip-finish tools, which come with instructions; use one if you like. Some tiers like them, I don't.)

1. Execute the usual half hitch by slipping a loop of thread over the shank.

2. Lift up on the working side of the loop (the side nearest you) and release the passive side (the side away from you).

3. Pass the working side from hand to hand adding three thread-turns over the passive side. You must keep the passive side out in front of the hook's eye as you add thread turns, otherwise you accomplish nothing.

TECHNIQUES, TACTICS & TERMS

4. Close the loop as you would a half-hitch loop.

WINDING HACKLE

There are three basic ways to wind a hackle: palmer it, wind it as a collar, and wind it as a parachute hackle. Palmering is already covered in this section under "Palmered Hackle." Here is how to wind a hackle collar.

TWO-HACKLE COLLAR

Here we will tie a typical two-hackle dry fly, so stiff, bright dry-fly chicken-rooster neck-hackles (or saddle-hackles) are used (see section II, "Materials," page 5). Hackle-size must be appropriate to hook-size, which is best determined using a tool called a "hackle gauge" (see "Hackle Gauge" in section I, "Tools," page 4).

1. Strip the fibers from each side on the stem, from about the center of the stem down. Here is an unprepared hackle and another that is stripped and ready to be tied in.

2. Typically, the tail, body, and wings are completed before the hackles are tied in. Here is a dry fly with both hackles tied in. Wind tight thread-turns over plenty of bare hackle-stem, then trim the stems and advance the thread to just back from the hook's eye.

3. Clamp on your hackle pliers well up the tip of one hackle. Wind the hackle forward in consecutive turns. Just behind the eye, secure the hackle's tip with a few tight thread-turns. Remove the pliers from the hackle's tip.

4. Clamp the pliers onto the tip of the second hackle. Wind that hackle forward as you did the first, but zig zag it a bit as you wind it, to avoid

trapping fibers from the first hackle. Secure the second hackle's tip as you did the first. Trim both hackles' tips closely, and then create a thread head if one is appropriate (see "Thread Head" in this section, page 16).

ONE-HACKLE COLLAR

1. A one-hackle collar is easier to create than a two-hackle collar—just wind the hackle forward in close, consecutive turns. One-hackle collars are used on such flies as nymphs, streamers, soft-hackle flies, and dry flies. The type of hackle used in a one-hackle collar depends on the type of fly it is used in. Sometimes a feather other than a hackle is used; just use whatever the pattern calls for (see "Pattern" in this section).

PARACHUTE COLLAR

There is really no traditional method for creating a parachute hackle, so I offer my own. A parachute hackle is rarely used in anything but a dry fly, so it is normally created with a dry-fly hackle.

1. Tie in the wing about three quar-

ters up the shank, and set it upright as you would set a single wood duck or hair wing of a pair (see "Wings," in this section). Wind the thread lightly up, then down the wing's base in consecutive turns. By using light thread-tension, you can do this without having to hold the wing.

2. Hold a proper-size hackle, with its lower stem stripped, along the wing's base as shown. Wrap a *medium-tight* layer of thread up the wing's base (and stem); then wrap another layer down the base with even more thread-tension. Note that the wing's base became stiffer with each new layer of thread, in turn allowing more thread-tension with each succeeding layer.

3. Draw the stem back along the shank, secure it with thread, trim it.

4. Add the tail and build the body.

The thread should hang just back from the eye. Wind the hackle down the wing in close, consecutive turns to the body. Let the hackle pliers (and the hackle's tip) hang on the far side of the hook.

5. Draw the hackle fibers up and back from the eye. Secure the hackle's tip under tight thread-turns. Trim away the hackle's tip; then build and complete a thread head (see "Thread Head" in this section, page 16). Add head cement to the thread head. When the cement is hard, tug the hackles and wing into shape.

WING CASE

The wing case is a common component of an artificial nymph. It can be formed in a variety of ways; here is the most common:

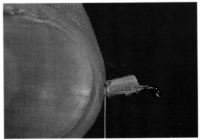

1. Secure the wing case fibers atop the shank (at the front of the abdomen, roughly the center of the shank) using a sort of modified pinch. Add a few tight thread-turns, trim the fibers' butts and bind them, complete the thorax, ending with the thread just behind the eye.

2. Draw the fibers up, and then forward and down. Secure the fibers with tight thread-turns at the front of the thorax. Trim the fibers and bind their cut ends with thread. Wing case completed.

WINGS

There are all kinds of fly wings. Wings that sweep back over the body (dry-fly down wings, wet-fly wings, bucktail wings, and streamer wings mostly) are tied in using the pinch; then the butts are trimmed and covered with thread.

SWEPT-BACK WINGS

1. Tie in most swept-back wings using the pinch. Add a few tight thread-turns; then trim the butts and cover their cut ends with thread-turns.

2. Clockwise from the top: a dry-fly

down wing of hair, streamer wing, bucktail wing, wet-fly quill wings.

HACKLE-TIP WINGS

Most upright dry-fly wings are tied in as a single bunch of fibers and then split and set upright. Hackle-tip and quill wings are handled with a different, though similar, approach. Since hackle-tip and quill wings are easier, we begin with them.

1. Hen-neck hackles are my favorite for hackle-tip wings, though almost any chicken hackle will suffice. Hold the hackles back to back, tips even, curving away from one another. Measure the tips along the shank (see "Proportions and Measuring" in this section, page 13).

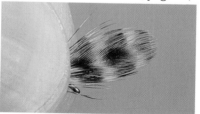

2. Tie in the tips using the pinch.

3. Normally, you would create the tail and body next. With that done, pull the wings back and down. Trim away the fibers that project forward.

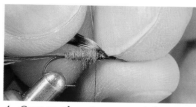

4. Crease the stems upright with your thumbnail.

5. Add tight thread-turns against the front of the stems to secure them upright. Wings complete.

UPRIGHT QUILL WINGS

1. For upright quill wings, begin by removing sections from matching left-right primary (quill) feathers. The sections should be no wider than the hook's gape (I prefer them a bit slimmer).

2. Hold the sections back to back, tips

TECHNIQUES, TACTICS & TERMS

even, curving away from each other.

3. Measure the sections against the hook (see "Proportions and Measuring" in this section, page 13). Tie in the sections using the pinch (usually, the long edges are down). Add a few tight thread-turns for security.

4. Generally, the tail and body are created next. With that done, pull the wings back and crease them at their base with your thumbnail; then add tight thread-turns at the front of the wings' base to secure them upright (as described previously for upright hackle-tip wings).

WOOD-DUCK WINGS

Next, upright wood-duck wings. Once you've got these, you will have an easy time with upright hair wings.

1. Here are two wood-duck feathers.

The one on the left is untampered with. The one on the right has been stripped of the fluff at its base, and a gape-wide section has been stripped from each side. These stripped sections will become the wings.

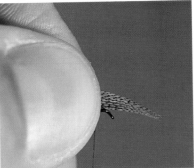

2. Hold the sections back to back, curving away from one another, tips even (review the previous two wing-types—upright hackle-tip and upright quill—if you are unsure about any of this). Measure and tie in the sections using the pinch.

3. Usually, the tail and body are created next. With that done, set the wings upright with a crease at their base with your thumbnail and tight thread-turns (for a review of creasing and thread-setting, see the previous two upright wing-types). Sight down the front of the wings, and then divide them with your scissors' closed tips. Pull each group of fibers firmly to its side.

TECHNIQUES, TACTICS & TERMS

4. Set the wings upright, one at a time, with thread, as shown in the illustrations. Here is a properly set pair of upright wood-duck wings. A common substitute for wood duck is dyed mallard.

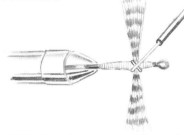

With the wings set upright and then divided to each side, take a few crisscrossed turns of thread between them.

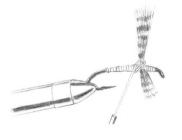

Bring the thread from the back of the wings forward between the wings, around the front of the *far* wing, then under it and back. Bring the thread toward you, over the shank behind the wing. Hold the wing and guide it upright as you pull the thread down. Release the wing and add a few tight thread-turns around the shank—you are

now wrapping the thread in the opposite direction from normal. The far wing should be set upright.

Pass the thread between the wings again and then around the near wing. Raise and set the near wing as you did the far one. Now the thread is back to its original direction.

UPRIGHT HAIR WINGS

1. Upright hair wings begin as a bunch of combed, stacked hair tied onto a hook using the pinch. The steps that follow are exactly the same as those for the wood-duck wings just described, except for one: After each hair wing is set upright, a few modestly tight thread-turns can be added around its base to group the hairs (see "Thread Direction and Tension" in this section, page 16).

TECHNIQUES, TACTICS & TERMS

KNOWLEDGE APPLIED

BRASSIE

BRASSIE
(created by Gene Lynch)

HOOK: Heavy wire, 1X or 2X long, sizes 10 to 20.

THREAD: Black 8/0 or 6/0.

ABDOMEN: Fine copper wire. (Option: a slightly larger-diameter wire for size-12 and -10 hooks. But the fine wire is easiest to work with, so use it at first.)

THORAX: Muskrat fur, dubbed. (Any gray fur can be substituted—rabbit, gray squirrel, or synthetic dubbing. See "Substitution" on page 16.)

COMMENTS: The Brassie usually imitates the pupa or larva of a caddisfly or midge or some other freshwater aquatic insect. (See "Pattern" on page 12 for information on reading a fly pattern.)

TYING A SIMPLE NYMPH: THE BRASSIE

The ever-reliable Brassie is very simple to tie, which is why you'll tie it first. If you run into problems or have questions concerning the Brassie or any other fly, refer back to "Tools" on page 4, "Materials" on page 5, "Pattern" on page 12, "Proportions and Measuring" on page 13, and "Components of Flies" on page 9.

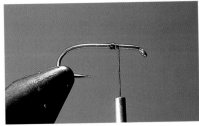

Step 1: Mount a hook in your vise (a size-12 hook would be good for a start). Start the thread about two thirds up the hook's shank. (See "Starting Thread" on page 15.)

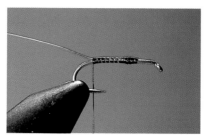

Step 2: Bind the end of some copper wire atop the hook two thirds up the shank, using the pinch. Hold the wire back as you spiral the thread down it and the shank to the hook's bend. (See "Light Turn" on page 11.)

Step 5: Trim a little muskrat fur from the hide (or use a substitute), and then spin the fur onto a couple of inches of the thread. Dub the front third of the shank to create a short, full abdomen. The thread should now hang between the thorax and the hook's eye. (See "Dubbing" on page 9.)

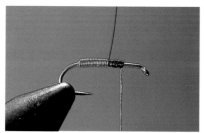

Step 3: Spiral the thread up two thirds of the shank. Wind the wire forward, each new turn diectly in front of the last, up two thirds of the shank.

Step 6: Build a thread head, whip finish and trim the thread, add head cement to the thread head with the point of a toothpick or a tool called a "bodkin," a needle mounted in a handle. (See "Thread Head" on page 16, "Whip Finish" on page 17, and "Cements" on page 5.)

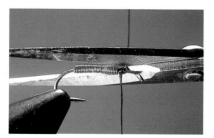

Step 4: Bind the wire there (two thirds up the shank). Trim the wire's stub end. (Cut hard materials, like wire, deep into the scissors, to protect their fine tips.)

KNOWLEDGE APPLIED

WOOLLY BUGGER

WOOLLY BUGGER
(created by Russell Blessing)

HOOK: Heavy wire, 3X to 4X long, sizes 14 to 2.

THREAD: Three-ought of a color similar to the body's color.

TAIL: One marabou plume of the body's color. The tail should be no shorter than the hook's shank, no longer than the hook's total length.

HACKLE: One hackle, to match or complement the body's color. Use a saddle hackle or big, long, soft dry-fly hackle.

BODY: Chenille in black, brown, olive, white—almost any color.

COMMENTS: In its vast diversity of colors and sizes, the Woolly Bugger catches just about any fish that will take a fly—trout, bass, pan fish, pike, salt-water species... Generally, it imitates nothing in particular, just looking instead like something big and alive.

TYING A SIMPLE STREAMER: THE WOOLLY BUGGER

With the Woolly Bugger you'll learn the pinch, how to handle chenille, and how to wrap a palmered hackle.

Step 1: Start the thread three quarters up the hook's shank. Measure a single marabou plume and then, using the pinch, bind it where you started the thread. (Before binding on the plume, try stroking a little water into it first, for control.) Hold the plume back as you spiral the thread down it and the shank to the bend. (See "Starting Thread" on page 15 and "Pinch" on page 12.)

Step 2: Trim the butt of the plume closely. Spiral the thread up to where you started it. Strip the fibers from the base of a long hackle's stem. Using the pinch, bind the stem to the hook's shank. Hold the feather back as you spiral the thread down the stem and shank to the hook's bend. Trim the stem. (See "Pinch" on page 12.)

Step 5: Clamp the tip of the hackle in hackle pliers. Wind the hackle up the body in five to seven turns. Bind the tip of the hackle; then trim it. (See "Palmered Hackle" on page 12.)

Step 3: Spiral the thread three quarters up the hook's shank. Bind some chenille along the shank to the bend. Trim the end of the chenille. Spiral the thread up almost to the hook's eye.

Step 6: Build a thread head. Whip finish the thread and trim it. Add head cement to the thread head. (See "Thread Head" on page 16, "Whip Finish" on page 17, and "Cements" on page 5.)

Step 4: Wind the chenille in close turns up to just short of the hook's eye—but do leave a little room in which to bind the chenille and, later, to form a thread head. Bind the chenille; then trim it closely.

GOLD RIBBED HARE'S EAR

─GOLD RIBBED HARE'S EAR─

HOOK: Heavy wire, 1X or 2X long, sizes 18 to 8.

THREAD: Brown 8/0 or 6/0.

WEIGHT: Lead or lead-substitute wire, usually under the thorax only.

TAIL: Guard hairs from a hare's mask, or substitute fibers from a body-feather.

RIB: Fine oval (or flat) gold tinsel.

ABDOMEN: Hare's mask fur, dubbed.

WING CASE: Mottled turkey primary.

THORAX: Hare's mask fur, dubbed.

COMMENTS: The Gold Ribbed Hare's Ear imitates a mayfly nymph, but it's well-known as a good all-purpose nymph for trout streams.

TYING A TYPICAL NYMPH: THE GOLD RIBBED HARE'S EAR

Here you'll learn to create a rib, common in many kinds of fly patterns; and a wing case, common in nymphs.

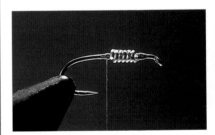

Step 1: Start the thread at the center of the hook's shank. Wind a short layer of lead wire over the front half of the shank, but stopping well back from the hook's eye (as in the photo). Trim the ends of the lead (but not with the scissors' fragile tips). (See "Starting Thread" on page 15, and "Lead" on page 11.)

Step 2: Trim some fur from a hare's mask, and then bind it to the hook's shank using the pinch. Hold the fibers back and spiral the thread down them and the shank to the hook's bend. Trim the butts of the fibers, if necessary. Bind the end of some gold tinsel to the shank at the rear of the lead, using a light turn. Hold the tinsel back, and then spiral the thread down tinsel and shank to the bend. (See "Pinch" on page 12, and "Light Turn" on page 11.)

Step 5: Bind a section of turkey primary (about as wide as the hook's gape, or slightly slimmer) atop the lead-wrappings, in front of the abdomen. Trim the butts of the turkey closely. Dub a thick thorax from the abdomen to just short of the hook's eye. (See "Wing Case" on page 20.)

Step 3: Dub a tapered abdomen to the middle of the hook's shank. (See "Dubbing" on page 9.)

Step 6: Draw the turkey forward over the thorax and bind it just behind the hook's eye. Closely trim the end of the turkey. Build a thread head, whip finish and trim the thread, coat the head with head cement. (See "Thread Head" on page 16, "Whip Finish" on page 17, and "Cements" on page 5.)

Step 4: Spiral the tinsel forward as four to six ribs. Bind the tinsel at the front of the abdomen; trim its end. (See "Ribbing" on page 14.)

KNOWLEDGE APPLIED

ADAMS

ADAMS
(created by Leonard Halladay)

HOOK: Light wire, standard length to 1X long (standard dry-fly hook), sizes 18 to 10.

THREAD: Black 8/0 or 6/0.

WINGS: Grizzly hackle-tips. (My favorite is hen-neck hackle, shown in the photographs, but some dry-fly neck-hackles are good.)

TAIL: Brown and grizzly hackle-fibers.

BODY: Muskrat, or gray synthetic dubbing.

HACKLE: One grizzly, one brown.

COMMENTS: The Adams is primarily an imitation of a mayfly and, when twitched or skimmed, of an active caddisfly. But when the choice of a dry fly is open, a lot of fly fishers reach for an Adams. What better testimony to the faith it inspires?

TYING A DRY FLY: THE ADAMS

"If I could fish only one dry fly, it would be the Adams," many fly-fishers would say. So I followed out that logic in selecting it as our sample dry fly; in other words: If you can tie only one dry fly (at first), let it be the Adams.

New techniques: with the Adams you'll learn to create upright wings and a dry-fly hackle collar.

Step 1: Start the thread about three quarters up the hook's shank, and then measure and bind on two hackle-tips there as wings. Trim the butts of the hackle-tips. (See "Starting Thread" on page 15, "Hackle-Tip Wings" under "Wings" on page 20, "Proportions and Measuring" on page 13.)

Step 2: Strip some long fibers from a brown and a grizzly hackle. Mix the fibers a little; then measure them and bind them along the shank as a tail. (See "Pinch" on page 12 and "Proportions..." on page 13.)

Step 5: Using a hackle gauge, find one brown and one grizzly hackle appropriate for the size of your hook. Prepare the hackles and bind them at the front of the body as described under "Two-Hackle Collar" on page 18. (See also "Hackle Gauge" on page 4.)

Step 3: With the thread at the bend, dub a tapered body halfway, or slightly past halfway, up the hook's shank. (See "Dubbing" on page 9.)

Step 6: Wind and then bind the tip of one hackle, then the other, as described under "Two-Hackle Collar" on page 18. Trim off the hackles' tips. Build a tapered thread head, whip finish the thread and trim it, add head cement to the whip finish. (See "Thread Head" on page 16, "Whip Finish" on page 16, and "Cements" on page 5.)

Step 4: Set the wings upright, as described under "Hackle-Tip Wings," in "Wings" on page 20.

KNOWLEDGE APPLIED

KNOWLEDGE APPLIED

BASS BUG

STANDARD BASS BUG

HOOK: Heavy wire, very short shank (standard bass-fly hook).
THREAD: For the tail: 3/0; very heavy thread for the hair. (See "Spinning Hair" on page 14.)
TAIL: Buck tail (or hackles or rubber-strand, whatever).
BODY: Deer or elk hair, any color, but usually with a white face.
COMMENTS: Though normally for largemouth bass, the bass bug can be very good for smallmouth bass too. On small hooks it's a fine fly for fresh-water pan fishes.

TYING A BASS BUG

Most floating flared-hair bass bugs are just that: "bass bugs." No individual titles for all the options and minor variations. If it has a plump body of flared and shaped hair and some sort of tail, it's just a bass bug, regardless of whether or not it has eyes, rubber-strand legs, or any other likely addition.

Flaring and shaping hair is common practice in tying both floating and sinking bass flies of all sorts; in fact, it's become a big part of tying in general, for trout, salt-water species, steelhead, and just about any fish a fly might interest.

Step 1: Start the 3/0 thread about one quarter of the way up the hook's shank. Cut a bunch of hair from a buck tail. Comb out the butts of the hair; then stack it in a hair stacker. (See "Spinning Hair" on page 14 and "Hair Stacker" on page 4.)

Step 4: Spin and compress bunches of deer hair up the hook's shank to its eye. Note that the front bunch of hair is white; this makes the fly easier to spot on the water. (See "Spinning Hair" on page 14.)

Step 2: Starting with a light turn, bind the hair along the rear quarter of the shank, as a tail. The tail should be about one and a half times the full length of the hook. Trim the butts of the hair closely. (See "Light Turn" on page 11.)

Step 3: Whip finish, then trim the thread just ahead of the tail. Start a heavy hair-spinning thread over the whip finish in the 3/0, directly in front of the tail's butts.

Step 5: Whip finish the thread at the hook's eye (or add a few half hitches instead). Trim the thread. Trim the hair to the shape in the photograph on page 32. (Notice that the hair on the rear of the finished bass bug on page 32 is trimmed well forward, exposing the 3/0 thread-turns holding the tail. I suggest you trim the hair there with scissors—a razor blade might cut the 3/0 thread and ruin the fly—or trim the rear of the body back further, past the 3/0 thread-turns.) Add head cement to the whip finish. (See "Half Hitch" on page 11, and "Shaping Spun Hair" on page 14.)

BIRD'S STONEFLY NYMPH (NYMPH)　　　CAL BIRD

HOOK: Heavy wire, long shank (curved shank shown), sizes 10 to 4.
THREAD: Orange 6/0 or 3/0.
WEIGHT: Lead wire.
TAILS: Dyed-brown goose biots.
RIB: Orange floss or heavy thread.

ABDOMEN: Brown rabbit.
WING CASE: Mottled turkey.
HACKLE: One, brown, palmered.
THORAX: Peacock herl.
COMMENTS: For imitating a big stonefly nymph or all-around use.

CLOUSER DEEP MINNOW (STREAMER)　　BOB CLOUSER & LEFTY KREH

HOOK: Heavy wire, 3X or 4X long, sizes 10 to 4.
THREAD: Dark 3/0.
EYES: Lead barbell.
BELLY: White buck tail, bound both behind and in front of the eyes.
WING: Dark buck tail over gold

Krystal Flash or Flashabou, bound at the hook's eye only.
COMMENTS: Fresh water, salt water, trout, bass, bonefish—a versitile streamer. (Especially good, in my opinion, for smallmouth bass.) Usually tied in dark fish-colors.

DAVE'S EELWORM STREAMER (BASS STREAMER) DAVE WHITLOCK

HOOK: Heavy wire, long shank, sizes 4 to 1/0.
THREAD: Three-ought or heavier.
EYES: Silver bead-chain, mounted beneath the hook's shank.
WEIGHT: Lead wire (optional).

TAIL: Four long, dyed grizzly hackles inside two shorter ones.
HACKLE: One, palmered.
BODY: Natural fur dubbing.
COMMENTS: A fine largemouth-bass streamer. Any dark color.

ELK HAIR CADDIS (DRY FLY)   AL TROTH

HOOK: Light wire, 1X long (standard dry-fly hook), sizes 18 to 8.
THREAD: Tan 3/0.
RIB: Fine gold wire.
BODY: Hare's mask.
HACKLE: One, brown.

WING: Bleached elk hair.
COMMENTS: Palmer the hackle *back,* from the front of the body to the hook's bend; then spiral the wire *forward* through the hackle. Time-tested caddisfly dry fly.

FOAM ANT (DRY FLY)

HOOK: Light wire, 1X long (standard dry-fly hook), sizes 20 to 14.
THREAD: Black or tan 8/0 or 6/0.
BODY: A cylinder or strip of black or tan closed-cell foam.
INDICATOR: Yellow poly yarn.
HACKLE: One, the body's color.

COMMENTS: Buoyant closed-cell foam has been catching on among fly tiers for a couple of decades. Foam flies range from pure simplicity (like the Foam Ant) to complex and realistic.

LEFTY'S DECEIVER (STREAMER)   LEFTY KREH

HOOK: Heavy wire, short to standard length (corrosion-resistant for salt water), medium to *big.*
THREAD: Dark 3/0.
TAIL: Six to ten saddle hackles inside Flashabou or Krystal Flash.
CHEEKS: Buck tail.

TOPPING: Peacock herl, or dark buck tail, Flashabou, or Krystal Flash.
THROAT: Red Flashabou or such.
EYES: Painted on and coated with head cement (optional).
COMMENTS: A standard salt-water streamer. Many variations.

LIGHT CAHILL (WET FLY)

DAN CAHILL

HOOK: Heavy wire, regular length to 1X long, sizes 16 to 10.
THREAD: Cream 8/0 or 6/0.
TAIL: Wood-duck flank fibers.
BODY: Cream fur (usually badger).

HACKLE: One, ginger (tan) hen.
WING: Wood-duck flank.
COMMENTS: Old-time wet flies, like the Light Cahill, aren't often fished now, but they still catch trout.

MIKULAK SEDGE (DRY FLY)

ART MIKULAK

HOOK: Light wire, 2X long, sizes 12 to 6.
THREAD: Eight-ought or 6/0 of the body's color.
TAIL: Natural-light elk hair. (The tail is actually part of the wing.)
BODY: Synthetic dubbing.

WING: Natural-light elk hair, in two or three bunches up the body.
HACKLE: One, brown.
COMMENTS: Dub some body, bind on a wing-bunch, dub... An imitation of a caddisfly adult, this is also a great all-purpose big dry fly.

PARACHUTE BLUE DUN (DRY FLY)

HOOK: Light wire, 1X long (standard dry-fly hook), sizes 18 to 10.
THREAD: Gray 8/0 or 6/0.
WING: One, natural-white calf tail.
HACKLE: Blue dun, parachute-style.
TAIL: Blue-dun hackle fibers.

BODY: Muskrat fur or any gray natural or synthetic dubbing.
COMMENTS: This is just the standard Blue Dun but with a single wing and parachute hackle. Many parachute flies are just standard dry flies converted. Others aren't.

PARTRIDGE AND ORANGE (SOFT-HACKLE FLY)

HOOK: Heavy wire, standard length to 1X long, sizes 18 to 10.
THREAD: Orange 8/0 or 6/0.
ABDOMEN: Orange floss.
THORAX: Hare's mask, short and full.

HACKLE: One, brown partridge flank or hen-saddle.
COMMENTS: A typical soft-hackle fly. Fished just under the surface, such flies can be deadly on trout.

PHEASANT TAIL (AMERICAN VERSION, NYMPH) AL TROTH

HOOK: Heavy wire, 1X or 2X long, sizes 18 to 10.
THREAD: Brown 8/0 or 6/0.
TAIL: Pheasant-tail fibers.
RIB: Fine copper wire.
WING CASE: Pheasant-tail fibers.

THORAX: Peacock herl. (Twist the herl and thread together—tougher.)
LEGS: The pointed tips of the wing-case fibers.
COMMENTS: A proven nymph, especially as a mayfly nymph.

RICK'S CADDIS (NYMPH) RICK HAFELE

HOOK: Heavy wire, 1X or 2X long, sizes 16 to 10.
THREAD: Brown 8/0 or 6/0.
WEIGHT: Lead wire (optional).
ABDOMEN: Natural or synthetic dubbing in any caddisfly-color.

THORAX: Brown dubbing, natural or synthetic.
COMMENTS: This simple fly echoes the simple form of the caddisfly larva it mimics. Simple flies can be effective.

SMP (PAN-FISH FLY)

SKIP MORRIS

HOOK: Light to standard wire, 1X long, sizes 14 to 8.
THREAD: Orange flat waxed nylon.
EYES: Lead barbell or bead-chain.
BODY: Bright-orange synthetic dubbing, spun onto the nylon.
WING: An orange marabou plume over a yellow one.

COMMENTS: A quick-sinking fly for the fresh-water pan fishes— bluegill, crappie, green sunfish and the rest. Also good in all-black and all-purple.